AIRPLANES

and Flying Machines

Created by Gallimard Jeunesse
Illustrated by Donald Grant

A FIRST DISCOVERY BOOK

D0060674

Cartwheel
·B·O·O·K·S· ®

SCHOLASTIC INC.
New York Toronto London Auckland Sydney

This airplane is now boarding.
Passengers walk through the jetway
to the entrance of the plane.
The flight attendant is waiting there
to check their tickets.

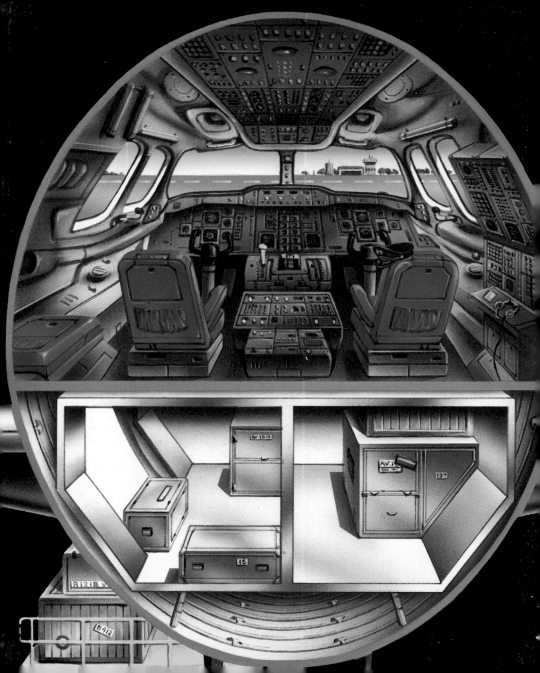

The cockpit is at the front of the plane.
The captain and the copilot sit in the cockpit.
They put on headphones and listen to
commands from the control tower.
Air traffic controllers will tell them
when to prepare for takeoff.

Luggage
is loaded into
the cargo bay
beneath the cabin.

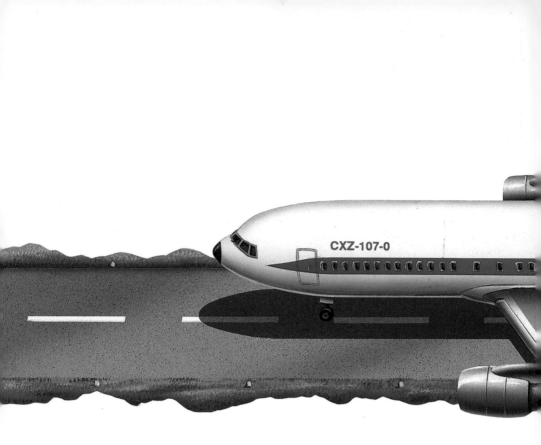

This airplane is more than 230 feet long.
Hundreds of people can fit inside!
They will travel far across the ocean
in only a few hours.

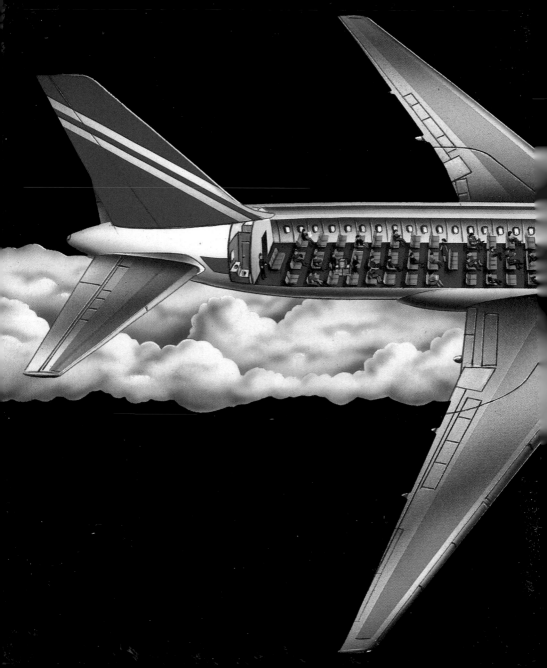

Two powerful jet engines and
sleek metal wings help the plane
fly high above the clouds.
Inside
the cabin,
the
passengers
watch a movie.
Even though the
air outside the plane
does not have
enough oxygen for
the people
to breathe, the air
inside the plane
is the same
as the air on the ground.

The Copilot

The Captain

The Flight Attendant

People have always been fascinated
by the idea of flying.   In 1783,

brothers Joseph and Jacques Montgolfier
invented a balloon that could fly.
It was lifted by hot air.
Its first passengers were
a sheep, a duck,
and a rooster!

Heaters
warmed the air that
filled the Montgolfier balloon.
Because hot air rises, the pressure from
the rising air lifted the balloon off the ground.

Because you couldn't steer a hot air balloon, no one could predict where it would land. This balloon dirigible was the first hot air balloon that could be steered.

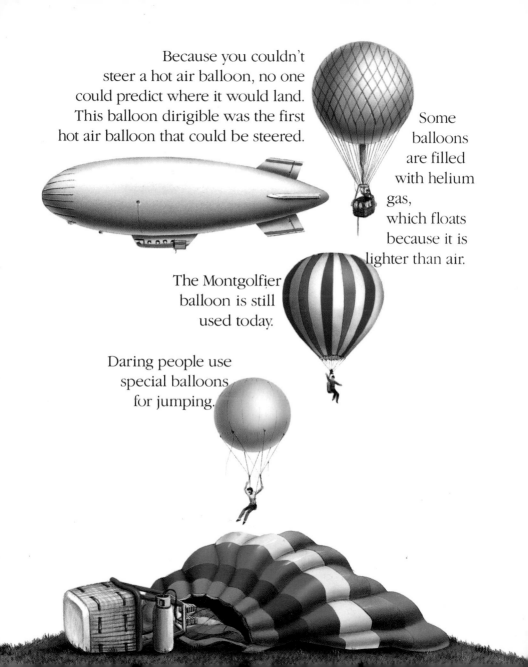

Some balloons are filled with helium gas, which floats because it is lighter than air.

The Montgolfier balloon is still used today.

Daring people use special balloons for jumping.

Wilbur and Orville Wright
built the first airplane that flew successfully.
Their first flight was on December 17, 1903,
near Kitty Hawk, North Carolina.

Some early fliers
made wings of cloth and wood
and tried to glide through the air like birds.
It didn't work!

This pilot had to pedal hard to keep the wings of his plane flapping. His plane flew 600 feet before it crashed.

World War I was the first war to be fought, in part, in the sky with fighter planes.

In 1927 Charles A. Lindbergh flew his airplane, the *Spirit of St. Louis,* across the Atlantic Ocean.

Planes of the early 1900s had only motors and propellers.

The first man to fly across the open sea was Louis Blériot. He flew across the English Channel from France to England in 1909.

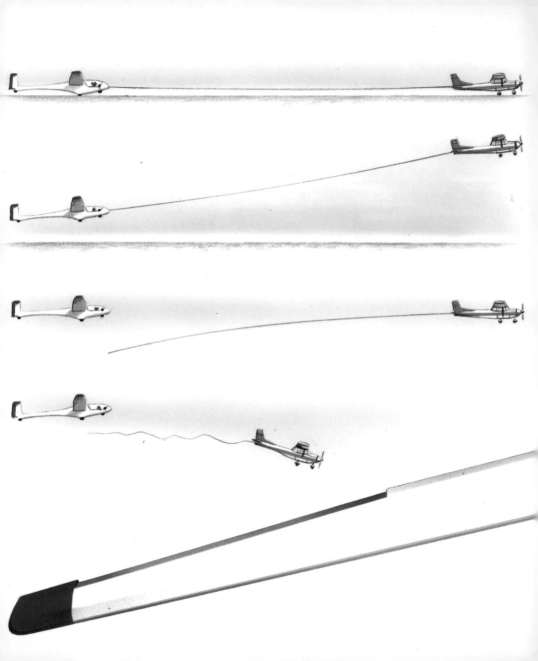

Gliders are planes
without motors.
A tow plane
must pull the glider
into the air.

The glider is attached to
the tow plane by a strong nylon rope.
When both planes reach about 3,000 feet,
the glider pilot pulls a release lever.
The rope snaps and the glider
soars on its own.

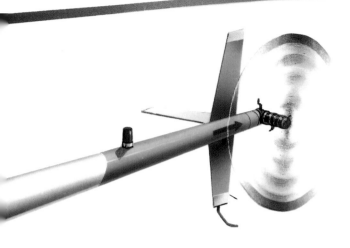

Helicopters can fly
straight up and down,
or they can hover in midair.

Helicopters don't need a runway to
take off or land as most planes do.
They can land on a roof, in a field,
or even on a ship!

These planes are very helpful!

The cargo plane carries trucks, cars, and boats over land and sea.

Fire fighters fill the tanks
of their planes with water...

then empty them over the burning flames
of a forest fire.

A helicopter sprays a farmer's orchards.

This man is going to
jump from the plane! His parachute
will help him land safely.

In the 1800s skydivers wore parachutes
to jump from hot air balloons.

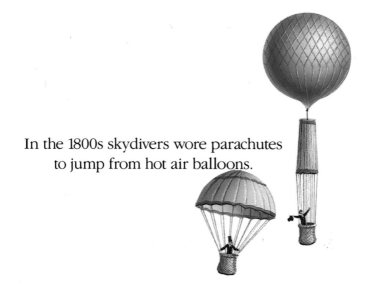

A parachute catches the air
to keep a diver from falling 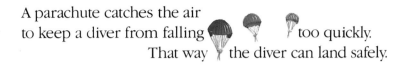 too quickly.
That way the diver can land safely.

Whee! A hang glider takes off from a cliff!

This glider has an engine. It took off from the beach.

The deltaplane's vast wings
make it the highest flying glider.

Hang gliding
is a sport
only the bravest
dare try!

Here's a glider built for two.

As a motorboat pulls the rope,
the parasailor sails up in the air!

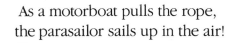

The Explorer plane can land
on water, snow, or land!

The Explorer can carry
five passengers comfortably,
along with a motorcycle and a raft!

Some model airplanes are powered
only by a rubber band!

Which would you like to fly?

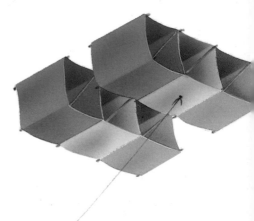

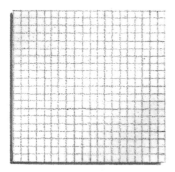
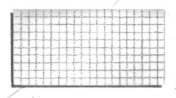
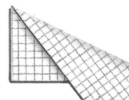

What a long tail this high-flying kite has!

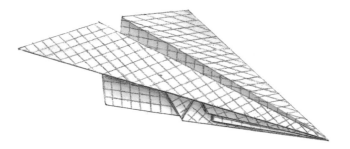

It's easy to make a paper airplane!

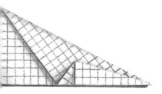

Take a square piece of paper.
Follow the pictures to fold the paper
and make your own high-flying plane!

Titles in the series of *First Discovery Books:*

Airplanes and Flying Machines

Bears

Birds
Winner, 1993
Parents Magazine
"Best Books" Award

Boats
Winner, 1993
Parents Magazine
"Best Books" Award

The Camera
Winner, 1993
Parents Magazine
"Best Books" Award

Castles
Winner, 1993
Parents Magazine
"Best Books" Award

Cats

Colors

Dinosaurs

The Earth and Sky

The Egg
Winner, 1992
Parenting Magazine
Reading Magic Award

Flowers

Fruit

The Ladybug and Other Insects

Light

Musical Instruments

The Rain Forest

The River
Winner, 1993
Parents Magazine
"Best Books" Award

The Tree
Winner, 1992
Parenting Magazine
Reading Magic Award

Vegetables in the Garden

Weather
Winner,
Oppenheim Toy Portfol
Gold Seal Award

Whales
Winner, 1993
Parents Magazine
"Best Books" Award

Library of Congress Cataloging-in-Publication Data available.

Originally published in France under the title L'AVION by Editions Gallimard.

No part of this publication may be reproduced in whole or in part, or stored in a retrieval system, or transmitted in any form or by any means, electronic, mechanical, photocopying, recording, or otherwise, without written permission of the publisher. For information regarding permission, write to Scholastic Inc., 555 Broadway, New York, NY 10012.

ISBN 0-590-45267-3

Copyright © 1989 by Editions Gallimard.
This edition English translation by Karen Backstein.
This edition American text by Nancy Krulik.
All rights reserved. First published in the U.S.A. in 1992 by Scholastic Inc. by arrangement with Editions Gallimard.

CARTWHEEL BOOKS is a registered trademark of Scholastic Inc.

17 16 15 14 13 12 11 10 9 8 7 6   4 5 6 7 8 9/9

Printed in Italy by Editoriale Libraria

First Scholastic printing, September 1992